Nonprofit Setup Simplified

An Essential Guide to Launching Your 501(c)(3) Charity in Record Time

Michele L. Whetzel

TWIN WILLOWS
PUBLISHING

Twin Willows Publishing

Dedication

This book is dedicated to my family and friends who have supported me through this amazing life. I especially want to thank my husband for loving and supporting me and making life so much fun! Thank you for being you.

Table of Contents

Introduction   1

Chapter 1   5
Name & Frame
   Key Naming Considerations
   Trademark Basics
   The Trademark Registration Process
   Intellectual Property: Trademarks, Copyrights, and Patents
   Domain Name
   Get Feedback & Reserve Your Name
   Official Email
   Doing Business As (DBA)
   Crafting a Powerful Pitch
   Chapter 1 Action Items

Chapter 2   17
Building Your Dream Team: Choosing the Right Board
   Set Up Your Initial Board
   Board Meetings & Policies
   Chapter 2 Action Items

Chapter 3   25

Determine If You Will Qualify

    Are You 501(c)(3) Ready?

    Chapter 3 Action Items

Chapter 4   29

Becoming Official

    Fiscal Year

    Articles of Incorporation

    Become Incorporated

    Chapter 4 Action Items

Chapter 5   35

Crafting Your Outward-Facing Identity

    Logo & Branding

    Website

    Database

    Chapter 5 Action Items

Chapter 6   45

Lock in Your Tax-Exempt Status

    Apply for the Employer Identification Number (EIN)

    Form 1023 or Form 1023-EZ?

    Chapter 6 Action Items

Chapter 7   51

Now Accepting Donations!

    Initial Account or Money App

    Bank Account

    Chapter 7 Action Items

Chapter 8   57

Announcing Your Nonprofit

Go Public

Congratulations!

Chapter 8 Action Items

Acknowledgments   61

Appendix 1   63
Elevator Pitch

Appendix 2   67
Sample Meeting Minutes

Appendix 3   73
Mission & Vision Statements

Appendix 4   77
Sample Articles of Incorporation

Appendix 5   87
Applying for EIN

Appendix 6   90
Sample Press Release

Resources   93

About the Author   95

Introduction

Have you felt called to make a difference, but feel overwhelmed by the process of starting a nonprofit? I have been there! I did not know where to start, but after a lot of hits and misses, I figured it out, and now I've laid it out here for you.

The first time I went through the maze of setting up a new nonprofit, I wanted to teach women in my state how to run a political campaign. The idea was to train women to help more of them get a seat at the table – whether on a local school board, running for a statewide office, or somewhere in between. There was a national organization willing to lend me their proven methods and expertise, but they required my organization to be a registered nonprofit to have access. That started me down the path of learning how to set up a nonprofit. How hard could it be? Well, after a number of wrong moves and lots of wasted time and frustration, I found my way. Knowing this would probably not be the last time I set up a nonprofit (it wasn't!), I kept good notes, so I wouldn't make the same mistakes the next time.

And now, here you are – ready to take that same brave step.

I want to say thank you! The fact that you are here, reading this, means you have a vision. A dream. A calling to serve others and make a difference in the world.

That is no small thing. It takes courage to turn a spark of inspiration into action, and I admire you for stepping up.

For this book, I am making the assumption that you have done some initial research to see if similar organizations already exist in your area. (After all, you don't want to duplicate services or compete unnecessarily for funding.) I also hope you have considered both the costs of setting up your nonprofit and the ongoing expenses of running the programs you have planned. Do you have a plan for securing funding? If you have not explored these questions yet, I encourage you to take a step back and do some deeper research before diving into the setup process outlined in this book.

Starting a nonprofit is not just about filing paperwork and checking boxes. It's about bringing hope where there is none, solving problems that others overlook, and creating lasting change in your community. If you feel that deep pull in your heart – the one that keeps you up at night imagining the people you could help – know that you are in the right place.

However, passion alone won't get your nonprofit off the ground. The process can be overwhelming, and I know that firsthand. When I started my first nonprofit, I stumbled through unnecessary obstacles, wasting precious time and energy, all while getting very frustrated. That's why I wrote this book – to make your journey smoother, faster, and less frustrating. Setting up a new nonprofit can take anywhere from a few months to a year, and I want to help you cut down that time significantly.

This is your roadmap. I'll walk you step-by-step through the essential process of launching your nonprofit the right way – from choosing a name and assembling your team to filing for tax-exempt status and setting up systems for long-term success. **If you follow the steps in the order I lay out here, you'll avoid**

common pitfalls, save valuable time, and set yourself and your nonprofit up for a strong, sustainable future.

To make things even easier, I've included templates for key documents like your elevator pitch, meeting minutes, and articles of incorporation. Plus, you will find links to all of the resources and government websites you'll need to get up and running – fast.

This book is focused on **getting you launched.** If you need a deeper dive into governance, policies, fundraising, or long-term sustainability, check out my other book *So, You Want to Start a Nonprofit, Now What?*[1] (It also lists alternatives to setting up a nonprofit that may be a better fit for your project.)[2]

---

1. Available on Amazon and IngramSpark

2. There are many alternatives to setting up a corporation and then obtaining 501(c)(3) status. You may want to consider how difficult it will be to set up, run, get funding for, and stay in good standing with the IRS requirements for a tax-exempt organization (see 501(c)(3) requirements in Chapter 3 of this book). It is also difficult to dissolve a nonprofit once it is set up. Some options instead: join the board or volunteer for a nonprofit doing work you admire, leverage the fiscal sponsorship of an already-existing nonprofit to run your program under their 501(c)(3) umbrella (so your program is still tax-deductible for the donor), open a donor-advised fund through a local community foundation or similar organization to give funds to nonprofit programs you choose, start a for-profit company and apply for B Corp certification (driven by both financial profit AND mission), put together fundraisers for programs you passionately believe in, or any number of other, possibly less difficult, options.

Once you have read this book, **please consider leaving a review on Amazon**[3] **to help others decide if this is the right book for them**. Amazon shoppers rely on honest reviews to help them make selections. You may leave a short written review, or you can rate it from 1-5 stars only (no writing involved). You may also leave your review under an alias, so you are free to give your honest opinion.

I would love to hear about your progress! Feel free to reach out to me through my website, **www.501Guide.com**, and share your success story. The world needs what you are building – so let's get started!

---

3. Get this link and others through the access link found at the end of each chapter.

Chapter 1

Name & Frame

*"*N*ames are powerful things. They act as an identity marker and a kind of map, locating you in time and geography. More than that, they can be a compass. "* – Nicola Yoon (from the book *The Sun is Also a Star)*

Creating a memorable and impactful name for your nonprofit is the first major step in setting the stage for your organization's success. Your nonprofit's name is more than just a label – it's the cornerstone of your identity, and it will be one of the most important decisions you will make.

Key Naming Considerations

Your nonprofit's name should clearly reflect its mission and purpose. Avoid a vague or overly abstract name that doesn't give a clear indication of your cause. Before choosing the name, also look into domain name availability. (See below.)

Think Big AND Long-Term. Your nonprofit may move to a different location later, so you may not want to name it after your current location. It could grow to add programs or additional locations, so consider a more all-encompassing name. The organization may grow into something you can't even dream of right now.

If you name the organization for the one program you are running at the start, you might find that name limits you when you want to add different types of programs later.

You may also want to steer clear of naming the nonprofit after yourself or a specific person you intend to honor. The organization should eventually take on a life of its own, so if you intend for it to exist far into the future, the name should be adaptable as the nonprofit grows into something different from what you can currently anticipate. If you name it to honor a specific person, the story many years down the road will still be about the namesake. Will it be cathartic to have to discuss that person in every conversation about the organization, or will it be emotionally draining? Maybe consider more subtle ways to honor them rather than naming the organization after them.

In addition to making sure the name reflects the mission and values of the nonprofit, you may also want to think creatively. Explore wordplay, alliteration, or creative combinations of words to come up with unique and catchy names. Consider using metaphors, symbols, or words that help people feel a connection to the organization. Many organizations that have been around for a long time went from a multi-word name to just initials (Kentucky Fried Chicken to KFC and World Wildlife Fund to WWF, for example), so you may want to consider what initials the name may be shortened to later.

I have found that ChatGPT[1] (or other artificial intelligence [AI] helpers) can assist with brainstorming when given the right prompts. You will need to give it details and parameters about the organization you envision. For example, you can type in the prompt space, "I am starting a new nonprofit that will be training young people for jobs in the banking industry. I want the organization's name to

---

1. www.chatGPT.com **(See direct link to this site and all others in this book (plus bonus information) at www.501Links.com/footnotes)**

reflect that we are working with underserved teens to help them become employable in the banking industry. Can you list 10 creative names for my nonprofit?" As soon as you type that in and hit "enter," AI will churn out ten potential names. If you find that the responses miss the mark on what your organization intends to be, consider responding with something like, "Thank you for those great ideas. I like number 4, but I want the name to also reflect that we will be providing internships for the teens. Can you give me 10 more name ideas with this new information?" You will see that, as you hone in on the details, AI will adjust. You may like parts of one name combined with parts of another name. This exercise is meant to help you brainstorm, not to do all of the work for you.

There are other important factors to consider when naming the organization. **You want a name that others can pronounce, spell, and remember.** Check to be sure the words you include in your name, whether in English or another language, do not have additional meanings that you do not intend. Your charity's name should fit with the goals of the organization.

Once you have a few names you are considering, research extensively to ensure the name you ultimately choose is unique and easily findable. Do an online search for the name alone, the name along with the type of service or services you will offer, AND the name along with your town, county, and/or state to see if there are other organizations that have similar names in your area. You can save yourself a lot of headaches, money, and time by avoiding a name that is already in use by an existing organization. If the other organization had the name first and is well known for that name, they will not want your organization causing confusion with their clients, donors, or potential customers. You can do a free search at the United States Patent & Trademark Office (USPTO) online.[2] Check to be sure no

---

2. Trademark Search: https://tmsearch.uspto.gov/search/search-information

other organization has a trademark for that name (or a very similar one). If there are any doubts, speak with a qualified trademark attorney.

Trademark Basics

If you start using a business or product name, tagline, or logo in your geographical area before another organization, you may have **common law trademark rights**. Unlike federally registered trademarks through the USPTO, common law trademarks are established simply by using a mark in commerce. You may choose to add a "TM" superscript after your name or logo, but the trademark is implied without it. The first organization to use a mark in a specific geographical area generally has the right to protect it within that region, even without formal registration. However, enforcing these rights can be challenging since there is no central registry to prove ownership. To maintain common law trademark protection, the mark must be continuously used in connection with your goods or services.

After incorporating your nonprofit in the state of your choice, you may choose to **federally trademark your name** to protect its use nationwide. Registering your trademark with the USPTO offers several advantages:

1. Your trademark will be **listed in the national database**, providing public notice to others searching similar names or logos.[3]

2. Registration establishes proof of ownership, strengthening your legal rights.

3. You gain the ability to file a trademark lawsuit in federal court if needed.

---

3. A search will find the name as part of a phrase but may not find it if it is embedded in a logo.

4. You may use the "®" symbol indicating your federally registered trade-mark.

The USPTO provides resources on the trademark process, including a helpful "Trademark Basics" page.[4]

The Trademark Registration Process

To register a trademark, you must file an application through the USPTO, which is available online. The standard filing fee starts at $350, though costs may vary.[5] Many applicants hire an attorney to assist with the filing and to **conduct a trademark search** to check for existing marks that could cause conflicts. While legal assistance can improve your chances of trademark approval, it does add to the overall cost. If the search reveals potential conflicts, you may need to consider selecting a different name.

Before pursuing a trademark registration, carefully weigh your financial resources and other priorities against the risk of another organization using the same or a confusingly similar name. The USPTO website, along with a consultation with a trademark attorney, will help you determine whether federal registration is the right step for your nonprofit.

It's important to note that certain descriptive or generic words are not allowed to serve as trademarks. Reviewing the USPTO's guidelines on acceptable and unacceptable trademarks can help you choose a strong, protectable name for your nonprofit, even if you do not plan to file for a trademark right away. If your

---

4. Trademark Basics: https://www.uspto.gov/trademarks/basics

5. Apply for a trademark: https://www.uspto.gov/trademarks/apply

organization is starting out small and and operating locally, you may find it best to delay trademark filing until growth or expansion makes it a higher priority.

Intellectual Property: Trademarks, Copyrights, and Patents

Trademarks fall under the broader category of intellectual property (IP), along with copyrights and patents:

- Trademarks protect names, logos, and other identifiers that distinguish an organization or brand.

- Copyrights grant creators exclusive rights over their original works (e.g., music, art, written works, computer programs, architectural drawings), allowing them to control how their work is used and distributed.

- Patents protect inventions, including products, processes, and machines, preventing others from making, using, or selling them without permission.

Just as you may trademark your name to protect your nonprofit's identity, other forms of intellectual property – such as music, artwork (including cartoon characters), or sports team mascots – often require licensing or special permission for use. Be sure to check with an IP attorney to ensure you do not find yourself on the wrong side of a cease and desist letter or even a lawsuit if your organization publicly plays copyrighted music or uses any protected images, logos, or artwork owned by third parties.

Domain Name

When you have narrowed down the options to a few names, check for available domain names to secure your online presence. A domain name is a string of characters someone types into a browser window online to reach a particular website. You can go to a site like GoDaddy[6] or Namecheap[7] to check on the different Uniform Resource Locator (URL) options. A URL is the web address people will type in to find you online.

Input the whole name you want in your domain with no spaces between words in the "Search Domains" spot. You may add an underscore or hyphen between words, but people will need to remember that detail to find you online, so the less complicated your domain, the better. You can then see which endings are available to purchase for that string of words. Most nonprofits end in ".org," but some end in ".com," ".net," or something else. Again, it is all about what makes you most findable. Some of these endings may cost you more than others, so weigh the options. The cost and availability of the domain name should also be a factor in the name you ultimately choose for your organization.

Pay close attention to what the words look like when all strung together in the domain name. Take "choosespain.com" for example. Is it "Choose Spain" or "Chooses Pain"? Can you see how those words run together in a domain name may be read differently? (If you come up with some fun "bad" domain names, please share them! [Nothing vulgar, please.] Use the "Contact Us" form at www.501Guide.com/contact-us)

---

6. GoDaddy.com

7. Namecheap.com

Consider legal requirements for naming in the state in which you incorporate the organization. You may need to choose from a list of words where one of these words is required to be in the name. Some of these may be "Association," "Fund," "Inc.," or "Incorporated." Also, "Foundation" may be one of the words the state allows, but I would steer clear of this word in your nonprofit because a foundation is a separate type of 501(c)(3) under federal law. (501(c)(3) is the IRS designation for certain types of tax-exempt organizations.) You do not want people to confuse your public charity with a foundation.

Get Feedback & Reserve Your Name

Once you feel you have THE name, share it with a small number of people you trust to get their feedback. They have different life experiences and may give you insight you had not thought about – for or against that name. Be open to their feedback at this stage (before it is too late in the process), and make adjustments if needed.

Most states offer the option to file a name reservation, allowing you to secure your chosen name for a couple of months – often for a small fee – until you are ready to officially register your nonprofit. This process is usually available on the same website where you file for incorporation. Since you have put in the effort to find the perfect name, it's wise to reserve that name as soon as possible. Otherwise, someone else may register the name before you do. If you let your registration expire before incorporating, that name is available for anyone to use.

Official Email

When you purchase your domain name, you may also seriously consider adding one to three email addresses under that domain. You could make one a more general "Info@yourdomain," one with your name ("JaneDoe@yourdomain"), and one for someone else who is active from the start. Many times the domain registry site will offer a package deal that includes the domain and a linked email address. Sending email from a professional name will lend more credibility than sending an email from a Gmail or other free email account.

Doing Business As (DBA)

Down the road, if you find a reason to have an additional name that will be operating under the same tax-exempt umbrella, you may file with the state for a "Doing Business As" or "DBA" name. A DBA name may also be referred to as a "fictitious business name," an "assumed name," or a "trade name." The purpose of registering a DBA name is to allow your business to operate under a name different from your legal name without creating an entirely separate legal entity. If your organization is growing, and you want to add a subsection that operates as a separate identity, you may want to register for a DBA. There is a nominal cost for adding a DBA, and it allows your organization to open a bank account and accept funds under this additional name to compartmentalize programs or branches of your organization.

A DBA can be added to both nonprofit and for-profit corporations. For example, when I first started my business I incorporated Revise Resume, LLC as an LLC for my resume writing services. Years later when I published my first book, my focus shifted toward helping nonprofits – something completely unrelated to resumes. Rather than setting up (and paying for) a separate LLC for this new venture, I applied for a DBA. Now my business operates as Revise Resume, LLC and Revise Resume, LLC DBA 501 Guide. This allowed me to open a separate business checking account in the name of 501 Guide, helping me keep income and expenses for both sides of my business organized and separate without the need for an entirely new legal entity.

Crafting a Powerful Pitch

With your name secured, it's now time to craft your impact narrative, also known as an "elevator speech" or "elevator pitch." You want your passion about this project to be contagious so others will get behind you. These people can be the early funders of your organization – and the cheerleaders going forward if they buy into your plan. You can have the best idea for a charity, the proper passion and purpose, and even a great need for the services you will offer, but if you do not have enough community support, the charity may struggle to succeed. There is so much competition out there for resources like funding and volunteers. If your nonprofit is not a priority in your community, you will be constantly running behind other similar organizations in gathering time, talent, and treasure.

Your elevator speech should be concise, compelling, and memorable – capturing your organization's mission, impact, and vision. This should be a memorized two- or three-minute pitch that gives a quick overview of why the organization exists. Is it in memory of a person? Include a quick, moving story as to why you want to honor them. You will also want to include:

~ Who the organization intends to serve and how,
~ The need you know is out there for these services,
~ How you will reach the intended target(s),
~ Any funding or backing you currently have, and
~ Your long-term vision for addressing the problem(s).

Type or write the details, then edit and wordsmith until it is short and to the point but with enough details and tug-at-the-heartstrings information for people to remember you and your nonprofit. Memorize the longer version, but also have alternate versions in mind to fit in longer or shorter discussion times as needed. Think about three key takeaways you want everyone to have, even if you only have

30 seconds in an elevator to make your pitch. Remember that your narrative will evolve over time as your organization grows and changes.

Try the pitch out on people in the community who you trust to give you honest feedback. Ask them for advice on what they see as potential barriers to success and how they suggest overcoming them. Ask them who else you should speak to about your program and ideas. I have found that people are very willing to help if you ask for their opinion (everyone has one!) rather than asking for their money or sweat equity. However, once you get them invested with their feedback and opinions, there is a good chance they will be a supporter in other ways going forward. There is a sample Elevator Speech in Appendix 1.

Chapter 1 Action Items

~ Brainstorm names for your organization.

~ Consult a few trusted people to get feedback on names you are considering.

~ Research then purchase your domain name (once you are sure of the name).

~ Craft your elevator speech.

~ Test your pitch, gather feedback, and adapt as needed.

~ Go to www.501Links.com/footnotes to get clickable links to all footnotes.

Chapter 2

Building Your Dream Team: Choosing the Right Board

————◆◇◆————

"We must remember that one determined person can make a significant difference, and that a small group of determined people can change the course of history." - Sonia Johnson

Set Up Your Initial Board

A nonprofit organization is directed and overseen by its board of directors. As the founder, it's crucial that you put together a diverse and passionate board from the beginning.

State and federal laws require that a nonprofit organization be governed by a board of directors. When you apply for your nonprofit status with the IRS, your initial board members (a minimum of three) must be listed on the application. This means the founder needs to start to form the board as soon as possible. Once the initial board is formed, the board runs the organization for the rest of the nonprofit's existence with the founder only having one vote on that board. You will want to establish term limits for board members to ensure fresh perspectives over time. As a founder, it's also important to develop an exit strategy, allowing the organization to transition smoothly to the next generation of leaders. Ultimately, a well-structured nonprofit should be able to thrive beyond its founder, sustained by a capable board and a shared commitment to its mission.

While it may be tempting for you, the founder, to put together a group of people you know and love who may be willing to follow your lead on all issues, the organization will be better and stronger in the long run if the board is diverse. **The board members will be unpaid volunteers.**[1] Make sure that is clear to anyone you recruit.

Your initial board will be small, so you will want a "working board" – those who have time to devote to get the organization up and running who you trust to be committed to this project. As your board grows, you want to aim for diversity in age, race, gender, expertise, life experience, and socio-economic status. People who have differing opinions and are willing to challenge the status quo can strengthen the organization's decision making, allowing the board to examine different options and ensure a broader perspective.

I recommend starting with at least five members including yourself, if you plan to be on the board. Look for individuals who are passionate and knowledgeable about the mission and are willing to contribute their time, skills, and dollars. Talk to people you believe would be a good addition and ask them directly if they would consider joining the board of your new organization. Give them the best

---

1. You want your board members to make decisions regarding the charity independent of their self interest. You do not want to have payments to board members affect the public's perception of your nonprofit or adversely affect your fundraising. Also, the IRS could revoke your tax-exempt status if they determine compensation of board members is beyond what is "reasonable."

version of your elevator speech to sell them on the mission. Whether they accept or not, ask them for recommendations of people they think would be an asset to your team. People have many reasons why they may not be able to serve as a board member themselves, but they may be willing to help you find others who will. If they recommend someone you do not know, ask them for an introduction to that person, then be sure to do some research to know a bit about the person before meeting them.

Seek out experienced professionals, individuals with general nonprofit and nonprofit governance experience, and even people who represent the community you wish to serve. Your nonprofit IS a business, so look for one or two seasoned business professionals.[2]

You are starting out with a skeleton board, but eventually you will also want to have people with good connections in the community (to get the word out and to attract other volunteers and donors). Look for people with nonprofit legal experience, nonprofit accounting expertise (like a CPA), financial competence, grant writing proficiency, and other skills that are directly related to the work your nonprofit does.

As your board grows, be mindful of situations where a single member represents a particular demographic group, as they may feel outnumbered or hesitant to voice differing opinions. If this can't be avoided, fostering an inclusive and welcoming environment is key to ensuring all perspectives are heard and valued. For your organization to operate at its highest level, every board member should feel empowered to contribute their unique skills, insights, and expertise – offering suggestions, questioning prevailing ideas, and constructively challenging decisions

---

2. You may also want to put together a business plan for the organization. See more about writing a business plan in *So, You Want to Start a Nonprofit, Now What?* by Michele L. Whetzel, pages 23 & 177.

when necessary. Of course, you also want "team players" who will express their opinions but will continue to work well with others even when their suggestions are out-voted.

You may want to consider having an odd number of board members to try to prevent tie votes. Also, put together a mechanism for overcoming a tie vote if an even number of board members attend a particular meeting or if one member needs to recuse from a vote due to a conflict of interest. Options you may consider: the board chair could cast the deciding vote, you could table the motion for discussion and vote at a later time, the bylaws could designate a specific board position to have the deciding vote (vice chair, governance chair, at-large member, etc.), or some other mechanism to break the tie.

You probably want to have staggered board terms, so not all board members are up for re-election the same year. This is also a good time to start discussing term limits for board members. The idea is to preserve some historical knowledge while also bringing in new members with fresh ideas.[3] It is common for nonprofits to allow board members to serve two- or three-year terms, with a limit of two or three consecutive terms before they are required to roll off the board for a year or two.[4]

---

3. Learn more about forming your board and board best practices in *So, You Want to Start a Nonprofit, Now What?* by Michele L. Whetzel, page 29.

4. For example: If the limits are three consecutive three-year terms, a particular board member may serve a maximum of nine years. A new board member would then take their place. Some nonprofits have three-year terms for board members but only two-year terms for officers. Do some research to consider your options.

The IRS requires a nonprofit to have three individuals serving as Officers and Directors for the organization, filling the roles of President, Secretary, and Treasurer. The President serves as the chief volunteer officer of the organization. The board Secretary is in charge of keeping the corporate records, taking meeting minutes, and giving notice of upcoming meetings in accordance with the bylaws. All financial affairs of the organization are overseen by the Treasurer. The Treasurer needs to pay close attention to detail, reporting (in a timely manner) on the financial position of the nonprofit, overseeing the budget and any employment records, and making sure all tax forms and other corporate filings are completed on time.

Initial board members should meet informally before the organization is incorporated. They may craft the mission and vision statements, discuss potential board members, and hammer out the details that will be written into the articles of incorporation. They may also decide on fiscal year dates, bylaws, and additional policy statements. Be sure the board members (or at least the majority needed to make decisions) are on the same page before incorporating, although votes at these early, informal meetings will not be official and do not need to be recorded. (We will look at preparing your articles of incorporation and filing for incorporation in Chapter 4.)

Board Meetings & Policies

Once the organization is officially incorporated (the incorporation certification is received from the state), the board will need to have its **first official meeting**. The first official board meeting should take place in person or on an online meeting platform not long after you incorporate. It is required that the board keep good records, called **meeting minutes**, of all board meetings, starting with the very first official meeting. Someone will need to take accurate notes of the topics discussed, any votes taken at the meeting, and meeting attendance. Eventually, this will be the duty of a designated board secretary, but, at the beginning, it can be a temporary volunteer. You will find sample board meeting minutes in <u>Appendix 2</u>.

A **quorum** is the minimum number of board members required to be present to take an official vote in any meeting going forward, so the decision as to what number or percentage of the total board constitutes a quorum for your organization will be one of the first items of official business upon which the board needs to vote. If a quorum is not present at a meeting of the board, no official votes may be taken or passed at that meeting. Other items to be voted on and adopted in the early meetings are the **mission and vision statements, the fiscal year dates, and your bylaws** once you have secured each of these.

The board should decide on the official wording of the mission and vision statements, bylaws, policy statements, and other important documents before voting on them. This may require forming a subcommittee of some of the board members to draft these items and then distribute the drafts to the board in the pre-meeting materials, allowing members to review and process the items before the meeting. Sending these materials out in advance ensures that valuable meeting time is better spent on meaningful discussion rather than reading through the documents for the first time. (It should be clearly communicated to all board members, especially the new ones, that they are expected to come to meetings prepared by reviewing the pre-meeting materials ahead of time.) Any suggested changes can then be discussed and finalized. Once a consensus is reached, the board can proceed with a formal vote to adopt the item.

Very early in the organization's existence, care should be taken to set up safeguards to ensure board members are good stewards of donors' funds. Checks and balances should be built into all that you do. Put processes in place that require a different person for each step of the money trail. You want to believe that all who handle valuables in your organization will do the right thing, but people are human, and there are all sorts of reasons people are tempted, especially if the lack of procedures makes following through on that temptation easy. Banking is often done online. Be careful who you trust with access to these accounts. You may also want to require authorization of two board members before making an online transfer or payment as an extra measure of security.

There is more about mission and vision statements in <u>Appendix 3</u>.

Chapter 2 Action Items

~ Recruit initial board members.

~ Hold informal board meeting(s) to discuss important formation documents.

~ The first official board meeting, with meeting minutes to record votes, important topics discussed, and meeting attendance, should be held not long after incorporation.

~ Go to www.501Links.com/footnotes to get clickable links to all footnotes.

Chapter 3

Determine If You Will Qualify

"*A ct as if what you do makes a difference. It does.*" - William James

Are You 501(c)(3) Ready?

The IRS recognizes various types of 501 tax-exempt organizations, but a 501(c)(3) is unique in that it is exempt from federal taxes and donations made to it are tax-deductible for the donors (to the extent of the law). Due to these benefits, the IRS imposes strict eligibility requirements for obtaining and maintaining 501(c)(3) status. Before you proceed further, it's important to determine if your organization qualifies for tax-exempt status with the IRS. You do not want to go through the process of incorporating only to find that you will not be able to create the charitable organization of your dreams.[1]

---

1. Exemption Requirements:

    https://www.irs.gov/charities-non-profits/charitable-organizations/exempt
    ion-requirements-501c3-organizations

Requirements:

1. The organization must be organized and operated exclusively for exempt purposes (see details in next paragraph), and none of the earnings may benefit any private interests, such as the founder or founder's family, shareholders of the organization, or other designated individuals.

"The exempt purposes set forth in section 501(c)(3) are charitable, religious, educational, scientific, literary, testing for public safety, fostering national or international amateur sports competition, and preventing cruelty to children or animals. The term charitable is used in its generally accepted legal sense and includes relief of the poor, the distressed, or the underprivileged; advancement of religion; advancement of education or science; erecting or maintaining public buildings, monuments, or works; lessening the burdens of government; lessening neighborhood tensions; eliminating prejudice and discrimination; defending human and civil rights secured by law; and combating community deterioration and juvenile delinquency."[2]

2. **This may not be an "action organization"**[3] that will attempt to influence legislation as a substantial part of its activities, and it may not

---

2. Exempt Purposes:
   https://www.irs.gov/charities-non-profits/charitable-organizations/exempt
   -purposes-internal-revenue-code-section-501c3

3. Restriction of Political Campaign Intervention:
   https://www.irs.gov/charities-non-profits/charitable-organizations/restrict
   ion-of-political-campaign-intervention-by-section-501c3-tax-exempt-organ
   izations

participate in any campaign activity for or against particular political candidates.

The IRS website says, "Under the Internal Revenue Code, all section 501(c)(3) organizations are absolutely prohibited from directly or indirectly participating in, or intervening in, any political campaign on behalf of (or in opposition to) any candidate for elective public office. Contributions to political campaign funds or public statements of position (verbal or written) made on behalf of the organization in favor of or in opposition to any candidate for public office clearly violate the prohibition against political campaign activity. Violating this prohibition may result in denial or revocation of tax-exempt status and the imposition of certain excise taxes.

Certain activities or expenditures may not be prohibited depending on the facts and circumstances. For example, certain voter education activities (including presenting public forums and publishing voter education guides) conducted in a non-partisan manner do not constitute prohibited political campaign activity. In addition, other activities intended to encourage people to participate in the electoral process, such as voter registration and get-out-the-vote drives, would not be prohibited political campaign activity if conducted in a non-partisan manner.

On the other hand, voter education or registration activities with evidence of bias that (a) would favor one candidate over another; (b) oppose a candidate in some manner; or (c) have the effect of favoring a candidate or group of candidates, will constitute prohibited participation or intervention."

If you find that some of what you had planned does not qualify for tax-exempt status, you may want to revisit your plan and amend it before going further. You want to be sure your organization meets the requirements for 501(c)(3) status to avoid complications later. You do not want to go through all of the steps, only to lose your tax-exempt status down the road because you have not complied with IRS regulations.

Once you are certain your organization will qualify, you can confidently move on to the next steps.

Chapter 3 Action Items

~ Look at the IRS requirements for a tax-exempt organization.
~ Compare the nonprofit you have envisioned to these requirements to be certain you qualify.
~ Go to www.501Links.com/footnotes to get clickable links to all footnotes.

Chapter 4

Becoming Official

—◄◆O◆►—

"The power for creating a better future is contained in the present moment: You create a good future by creating a good present." - Eckhart Tolle

You have now chosen a great name for your nonprofit (and have reserved that name in the state in which you intend to incorporate), you have memorized your elevator speech, and you have formed your initial board. Now it's time to become official!

Fiscal Year

Your first step in becoming official is to decide on your organization's fiscal year dates. These dates are required for the forms you will be filing and for your governing documents, and it will determine when your tax filings will be due each year. They also set the timeline for preparing your annual report that will keep your donors and the public informed. (This report highlights the impact of your organization's work, details how donations were used, and reinforces trust by showcasing your achievements over the past year.)

Some organizations run on a calendar-year basis but many choose their fiscal year to begin July 1 and end June 30. Others choose different dates that make sense for their organization.

Consider when your busiest time of year will be. This may be a bit of a guess this early in the process. Nonprofits do not pay federal income tax, but they do need to file their 990 forms[1] with the IRS on the 15th day of the 5th month following the fiscal year-end date. For example, if your fiscal year ends on June 30, your 990 form will be due on November 15, which means someone in your organization will be busy gathering the information needed to file starting at the end of October. If you anticipate this to be your busiest time of year, you may want to choose different fiscal year dates.

Articles of Incorporation

Next, you will need to prepare your governing document that will serve as the constitution of your corporation. Depending on the state in which you file for incorporation, this document may be called articles of incorporation, corporate charter, articles of association, certificate of formation, or certificate of incorporation. It is the charter that legally documents the creation of the corporation.

The document requires the name of the corporation and its registered address in the state in which you incorporate. It outlines your organization's purpose, details about how it may operate, information about the board and its members,

---

1. A Form 990 is an informational tax form that a 501(c)(3) nonprofit must file with the IRS annually. It provides an overview of the organization's activities, governance, and detailed financial information that helps the IRS ensure a nonprofit is not abusing its tax-exempt status. The form may also be used to share information about the organization with the public.

details about what must be included in the bylaws of the corporation and how those bylaws may be amended, and spells out what must happen if the corporation is dissolved in the future. A nonprofit has a "nonstock" charter because there will be no stock issued by the corporation, and no dividends or income may be distributed to directors, officers, or individual members except as reasonable compensation for services received by the corporation. ("Reasonable compensation" for board members of a nonprofit includes repayment for expenses paid on behalf of the organization. The organization may want to spell out the maximum dollar amount that may be spent without prior authorization by the board.)

You will find sample articles of incorporation in Appendix 4.

Be sure to consult the IRS website regarding articles of incorporation to ensure you have included all details necessary to be in compliance with tax-exempt requirements.[2] This may all sound a bit overwhelming, but you can look at the sample articles of incorporation to see the format, what should be included, and how it may be worded. The full document will end up being about five pages long. Try to find a local attorney in your area who is also passionate about your cause who may be willing to assist on a pro bono (free) or discounted basis.

Become Incorporated

With your documents prepared, it is time to file for incorporation in the state of your choice. You will form a corporation at the state level, and a little later, you will apply for your 501(c)(3) tax-exempt status at the federal level.

---

2. Required Information and Documents – Organizing Documents (Page 5):
   https://www.irs.gov/pub/irs-pdf/p557.pdf

Each state has its own requirements and processes for nonprofit incorporation, so be sure to research accordingly. You will need to adhere to the rules and laws of the state in which you incorporate, whether you have a physical location in that state or not. This means that you will most likely need to submit an annual filing with the state each year, and you may need to pay an annual fee when you file. In some states you will need to select a nonprofit startup corporation structure at the time of incorporation.

You may want to do your own online search to see where your home state rates in lists of the best and worst states for incorporating a nonprofit. Arizona, Delaware, Idaho, Montana, Nevada, Texas, Wisconsin, and Wyoming are usually at the top of the lists of states that are best for charities. This is due to factors like business-friendly environments, flexible governance, and lower costs.

I have prepared a document that gives information on how to file for incorporation in the eight states listed above. There will be a fee to file for incorporation in any of these states. The document also includes direct links to online resources for filing in those states. (See footnote 3 below.)[3]

It is common for a nonprofit operating in another state to be incorporated in one of these charity-friendly states, but it may be easier and more convenient for you to file for incorporation where you live and will do business. If you choose to operate in any state other than, or in addition to, the state of incorporation, your nonprofit must register with the appropriate authority **in each state** where you conduct fundraising operations, and you must also comply with that state's

---

3. You can find the document at www.501Links.com/incorporate.

nonprofit requirements. If you are located in or do a lot of business in a state with a sales tax, you may want to apply for a sales tax exemption in that state.[4]

Along with your application for incorporation, you will need to submit your board members' names and contact information, your articles of incorporation, and a registered agent's physical address – not a post office box. If you are a resident of the state, you can name yourself as the registered agent, but know that this means your address will be the legal address for the corporation until paperwork is filed with the state to change it. It is required that you have a physical location where someone can be available during business hours and where legal documents and correspondence may be received on behalf of the corporation. You may appoint someone other than you, the founder, but you want to be assured that they are a person who can be trusted with your corporate documents and nonprofit reputation.

There are registered agent businesses you may hire to be your statutory agent to receive legal notices, tax documents, and other notices on behalf of your organization. Their fees can range from $50 to several hundred dollars per year, depending on the services you choose and their location. Even if you are operating in the state in which you incorporate, there may be reasons to hire a registered agent. If you do not have a brick-and-mortar (physical) location, or if you expect to change addresses a few times in the early years, the registered agent can provide a permanent address for you. Their fee may also cover the federal and state filings due each year, and they can help you stay in compliance. Additionally, they can safely and securely hold your corporate documents. Some of the larger registered agent firms will also provide a wide range of startup-related services including

---

4. Here is a site that lists nonprofit state tax exemptions for all 50 states: https://www.harborcompliance.com/nonprofit-income-sales-use-tax-exem ptions-by-state

drafting formation documents, applying for the Employer Identification Number (EIN), and incorporation. Be sure you are hiring a reputable agency by doing a little research on them up front. This service will cost precious nonprofit dollars, so you need to weigh your options carefully.

Once you have filed for incorporation with the state of your choice, you will need to wait for the state's approval. This may take about four weeks, but in some states, it is possible to pay an additional fee for 24-hour turnaround. Once the state approves your documents, you will be sent confirmation of your corporation's existence.

In a number of states, it is required that, once approved, you publish your incorporation in media outlets deemed to be acceptable by that state. There may be certain required details such as publishing within 60 days of incorporation, listing the name of the organization, its address, the registered agent's address (if different), and details of the corporation. A list of the state's requirements should be included when you receive your confirmation of incorporation.

While you wait for your certification, you can work on your organization's outward-facing image, which will be covered in the next chapter.

Chapter 4 Action Items

~ Determine your fiscal year dates.

~ Choose the state in which you will incorporate.

~ Compose your governing charter.

~ Determine the registered agent (you, an agency, or someone else) and the registered address of the corporation (this must be a physical location, not a post office box).

~ Incorporate in the state of your choice and complete post-filing requirements.

~ Go to www.501Links.com/footnotes to get clickable links to all footnotes.

Chapter 5

Crafting Your Outward-Facing Identity

———◆◇◆———

"*D*esign is the silent ambassador of your brand.*"* - Paul Rand

  While you are waiting patiently for the state's stamp of approval of your corporation, you should start to set up the outward-facing pieces of the organization. Then, when your state and federal filings are confirmed, you will be able to quickly launch your public persona.

So far, you have been putting together the internal structure of your new non-profit. Now you will spend some time creating the parts you will present to the world.

Logo & Branding

Your logo is the visual representation of your organization's identity – the brand recognition for your charity. If you are creative, you may want to design the logo yourself, but there are specific sizes and file types that printers and web designers require. If you do not have enough familiarity with the graphic design specifications or do not have access to creative software, you may want to hire a graphic artist, or barter with one, to create a logo in exchange for sponsorship recognition or other advertisement at your events or on your website.

You may also consider a crowdsourcing site like Crowdspring[1] or Fiverr[2] where graphic designers bid to create a logo that matches your specifications. This can be a relatively inexpensive way to find a great design. I have also designed my own logo in Canva,[3] and you may want to do a search for free artificial intelligence (AI) logo creators since this field is changing every day.

When designing the logo, think about the colors you would like to use that will be associated with your brand going forward.[4] Try to choose colors that are traditional and not just trending at the moment. Think about the ease of duplicating your colors for branded items – promotional merchandise like a tablecloth for an event or aprons for volunteers. Also, consider how the logo will look if printed in black and white when you do not have the option to print in color.

---

1. crowdspring.com

2. pro.fiverr.com

3. Canva is a user-friendly, online graphic design platform found at: Canva.com

4. You may want to consider using Americans with Disabilities Act (ADA)-compliant colors in your logo. This means prioritizing high contrast between the color of your text and background, using tools to check contrast ratios, and avoiding color combinations that are difficult for people with color vision deficiencies to distinguish like red and green.

It's crucial to create a design that resonates with your mission. Use fonts that are easy to read. There are far too many "fancy" logos where the name of the organization is impossible to read. This defeats the purpose of a logo, which is to make your organization's brand easily recognizable and understood.

Think about whether you want to use graphics in addition to letters in your design. The logo must be as easily understood and recognized on a large banner as it is on a small brochure, so consider how the type and graphics will translate to different sizes, shapes, and formats. Determine whether the graphic will be easy to reproduce and how it may look if it is reproduced using a low-quality printer or copier. On some social media pages or in ads, there may be a size and shape requirement, so consider how the logo will look in square, round, oval, or rectangular spaces. Is there a way to fit only a piece of it and still leave it recognizable?

You may want to put together a small focus group to get feedback on logo options before you settle on one. Include marketing or branding experts as well as non-experts (everyday folks) to get different perspectives you may not have considered. They should focus on readability, how the logo relates to your mission, and even how it may look like something other than what you anticipated, intended, or were able to see on your own. Of course, you may pick and choose which suggested changes you adopt, then go back to the designer to make the revisions.

Your logo may change over time as your organization evolves, but you want to start with a logo and branding that people will come to recognize, know, and trust, that serves your nonprofit well for a long time. Rebranding can be expensive and time consuming because it means changing all printed materials, your website and social media platforms, signage, and other materials.

Website

Now that you have a logo, it's time to start creating your website. A professional website is essential for establishing credibility and reaching your audience. People will attempt to go to your website to learn more about you. If you do not have a website, or if it is outdated or looks unprofessional, it will reflect poorly on your organization. In many instances, the website is the first interaction people will have with your nonprofit, so you want to make a good first impression.

It is important to use a reputable, experienced website developer who can build a secure, compliant, and engaging website that includes best practices, security, and legal compliance. Some states require you to get informed consent before the visitor enters your site if you intend to capture some of their personal data when they visit.

You may be able to find a volunteer with website expertise to create your website, or you may be able to barter in some way where you arrange for a person to create the website in exchange for recognition of their business. If you don't know someone with that particular skillset, you will probably need to hire an expert.

Use a website platform and a web host that is secure. If you want people to find your website through Google or other search engines, you need to use modern digital marketing best practices like Search Engine Optimization (SEO). SEO is the process of growing a website's organic search traffic. The aim is to rank higher than similar organizations when someone is looking for the services you offer, so people will be directed to your website ahead of your competition's. This can be done by researching which keywords people search for, crafting website content that aligns with those keywords, and making sure your content is as clear as possible. This all starts with a domain name that fits with your organization, is findable, and is easy to recognize and trust.

Your website can be a very simple single page, or it can have multiple tabs, each with different types of information. If you have more than one tab, your landing (home) page should be short and to the point but friendly and welcoming. You do not want to overwhelm visitors with everything all at once. Give them a quick overview, your mission and core values, ads for upcoming events, and, of course, links for them to sign up for your newsletter or to volunteer. Your main call to action should be "above the fold," meaning that it shows up toward the top of the page and is one of the things people see as soon as they land on your website's home page. Some calls to action may be, "Donate Now," "Register for Our Upcoming Event," or "Sign Up to Volunteer." Of course, you only want one of these at the top of your landing page. You may want to include some photos of recent events that include some well-known members of your community if you have them.

Be sure to have your contact information on each page, including an email address and phone number where people can reach you if they have questions or want to get to know your organization better. Somewhere you should also post your mailing address because some donors prefer to mail donations or send them from a bank, investment, or charitable account. You should also make it clear at the bottom of every page that your organization is a 501(c)(3) nonprofit (after your IRS approval) and that donations are "tax deductible to the extent of the law." You may want to list your Employer Identification Number (EIN) somewhere on the donation page, since many employers require an EIN to provide matching funds for employee contributions. You do not want to leave that matching money on the table! (We will look at obtaining your EIN in the next chapter.)

All other pages of the website should be easily accessible through clearly-marked tabs at the top or side of each page or through links elsewhere on the page. Include an "About" page that gives a short history of how and why the organization was formed; your organizational structure; a list of board members, advisory council members, and staff members with their photos and short bios; and any other overview information about your charity. Other tabs may include information about your programs, your organizational policies, annual reports (once you have them), contact information for specific people or sections of the nonprofit, and job postings when you are hiring.

You may want to add a tab with details for an upcoming event with links to register, sponsor the event, or volunteer to help. Be sure to include all of the event details like date, time, and location. Hide or delete this tab a month or so after the event, so your website does not look dated if someone visits it months later. On this event tab and most of the others, be sure to include a "Donate" button to make it easy when visitors are inspired to donate after learning more about the great mission you are serving.

Before your website goes live, test to see how it looks in all types of formats. Most people will be looking at your website on their phone, so you want to be certain it is formatted to look good and make sense on a phone screen as well as a laptop or tablet.

Assign someone in the organization the task of keeping the website up to date, maybe checking it monthly and deleting old content. Your website may be the first impression a person has of your organization, so you want visitors to know you are on top of things. If you have a "Contact Us" form on your website, be sure there is a person in your organization charged with checking for submitted forms and responding to them within a day or two.

Take the time to establish your nonprofit's public persona, and you will be ready to make a lasting impact in your community.

Database

When you first start out, your "database" will most likely consist of one or more spreadsheets with contact information for everyone you need to track. It is very important to keep this information in an organized, easily-accessible format. You want to start compiling the names and contact information for all interested parties. This may include your board members, volunteers, donors, and prospective donors. All of this is very valuable information for your organization and should be treated as such. Save these spreadsheets on multiple computers or in the cloud to ensure preservation of this precious data.

Be sure all members of your organization are aware that this information is private, so it should not be shared with anyone outside the organization. It is an asset to your organization, and you do not want to lose donors because you released their contact information to someone who used it improperly.

One person in the organization should be the responsible party for maintaining a specific spreadsheet and updating all known copies, so you are sure you have the most up-to-date information at all times. Eventually, as your organization and contact lists grow, you will want to upgrade from spreadsheets to a Customer Relationship Management, or CRM, database tool.

For now, start one spreadsheet to list donors and prospects (a development list), and another to list board members and other volunteers, employees, and contractors you use.[5] There may be some overlap – for example, when volunteers also become donors.

---

5. There is a sample database spreadsheet in the Footnotes document at: 501Links.com/footnotes

Columns may include:

~ First Name
~ Last Name (you want to separate first and last for easy sorting)
~ Title (Mr., Mrs., Dr., etc.)
~ Company they work for or represent
~ Street address
~ City
~ State
~ Zip
~ Mobile phone
~ Additional phone
~ Email
~ Miscellaneous Information (any extra details you feel are important)

For the development list, add:

~ Gift date
~ Gift amount
~ Gift type (cash, check, credit card)
~ Event the gift was related to (if relevant)
~ Additional details

For board members, include the date they started on the board, the year their current term ends, and the year they need to cycle off the board if there are term limits. It is always better to collect as much information for each person as possible because you may want to run a report at some point to look at some of the details.

You should take a fair amount of time, maybe a month or two, to get your logo, website, and spreadsheets all set up and ready to go. The time you are waiting for your confirmation of incorporation should be long enough for you to have your unique logo and branding, a website that is a good representation of your organization, and your contact spreadsheets ready to go.

Next up: Become a Nonprofit!

Chapter 5 Action Items

~ Create your logo & branding. (You may want to outsource.)

~ Find an expert to start setting up your website.

~ Put together your database spreadsheets.

~ Go to www.501Links.com/footnotes to get clickable links to all footnotes.

Chapter 6

Lock in Your Tax-Exempt Status

───────●───────

"The secret of getting ahead is getting started." - Mark Twain

You are getting so close to having all of the necessary building blocks in place! You now have a great name, an initial board of directors, the articles of incorporation, and you have incorporated. These all give you a nice framework for your organization. You have also made progress with your logo and branding, have looked into purchasing your domain name, and are in the process of setting up your website. Now we will provide the final structural base of your nonprofit.

Apply for the Employer Identification Number (EIN)

Once you have received confirmation of your incorporation from the state, the next step is to apply for an **Employer Identification Number (EIN)**, which is similar to an individual's Social Security Number. This number is required for a nonprofit to open a bank account, apply for 501(c)(3) status from the IRS, and receive tax-deductible donations. Each business and nonprofit has its own unique number. Unlike a Social Security Number, a nonprofit's EIN is publicly shared and is a way to find proof that the nonprofit is a registered 501(c)(3) tax-exempt organization. If an employer has a matching plan for employees' charitable donations, they will require the EIN before making the matching donation.

You will go to the IRS.gov link[1] and follow the instructions to apply as a corporation. Read the important information and then apply for your EIN. You will be required to complete the application once you start the process, so be sure to have the details of the exact name of your organization and other required information in front of you before you start. See Appendix 5 for specific instructions on how to navigate this process. **If you do not complete the entire process in 15 minutes or less, the site will time you out, and you will have to start again.**

You will receive your EIN as soon as you complete the application. If you choose to receive an online letter, you can download and save it right from the confirmation page. Be sure to print it and save it electronically for your records because you will need this number for tax filings and other official business for the rest of the nonprofit's existence.

Once your EIN is secured, you are ready to tackle one of the most crucial steps in the process – filing for your 501(c)(3) status.

Form 1023 or Form 1023-EZ?

Now, you have finally reached the step you intended for your organization all along! The IRS recognizes more than 30 types of nonprofit, tax-exempt organizations, but only those that qualify for 501(c)(3) status will be able to receive donations that are tax-deductible for the donors. In order to receive this favorable tax treatment, the nonprofit must not deviate from its stated purpose or mission.

---

1. EIN Application: https://sa.www4.irs.gov/modiein/individual/index.jsp

You must first file IRS Form 1023 to apply for recognition of exemption from federal income tax under section 501(c)(3).

In Chapter 3 you determined that your nonprofit will qualify to be a tax-exempt organization. Now you will determine which version of the Form 1023 you will need to file, and then you will apply for 501(c)(3) status.[2] The version of the form required will depend on your anticipated gross receipts and assets[3] for the first couple of years. There is a Form 1023-EZ for smaller organizations and the more cumbersome Form 1023 for those that do not qualify for the EZ version.

Go to the IRS.gov website for "Instructions for Form 1023-EZ[4] and scroll all the way down until you see the spreadsheet with questions. Answer each question on the spreadsheet. If you answer "Yes" to any one question, you are not eligible to apply for exemption using Form 1023-EZ. You must apply on Form 1023. **If you answer "No" to all of the worksheet questions, you may apply using Form 1023-EZ.**

---

2. "Top Ten Tips to Shorten the Tax-Exempt Application Process"
   https://www.irs.gov/charities-non-profits/top-ten-reasons-for-delays-in-pr
   ocessing-exempt-organization-applications

3. **Gross Receipts** = all revenue received from all sources within a tax year before subtracting any expenses
   Assets = resources owned by the organization that have value including, but not limited to: property, buildings, vehicles, equipment, cash, investments, accounts receivable, art and collectibles, patents, copyrights

4. 1023-EZ instructions may be found at https://www.irs.gov/instructions/i
   1023ez

If you qualify for the EZ form, the instructions for completing the form are found above the worksheet that you just completed, and the code for the type of non-profit will be found below the worksheet. (See more details at the IRS.gov page "About Form 1023-EZ, Streamlined Application for Recognition of Exemption Under 501(c)(3) of the Internal Revenue Code.")[5]

For either option, you will need to set up an account at pay.gov and enter "1023" in the search box. This should bring up two options – one to apply for exemption from federal income tax under section 501(c)(3) using Form 1023, and the other using Form 1023-EZ. Click "Continue" for the option that fits the form you qualified for in the worksheet exercise.

Read the instructions on the next page, then click "Continue to the Form" and complete the application. **You will need to have a bank account number and the bank's routing number for an ACH payment or a debit or credit card number in order to submit the form.** This is a catch-22 here because until you receive confirmation of your 501(c)(3) status from the IRS, you will not be able to open a nonprofit bank account (more about this in the next chapter). You will most likely need to use personal funds to pay for this and the incorporation. **This is the only time you should ever mix your personal funds and the organization's funds.** As of the publication date, the fee to file Form 1023 is $600 and to file a Form 1023-EZ is $275. (These fees are subject to change, so be sure to check at IRS.gov before filing.)[6]

---

5. "About Form 1023-EZ, Streamlined Application for Recognition of Exemption Under 501(c)(3) of the Internal Revenue Code": https://www.irs.gov/forms-pubs/about-form-1023-ez

6. https://www.irs.gov/charities-non-profits/applying-for-tax-exempt-status

Once you have your nonprofit bank account, are officially a 501(c)(3), and are receiving donations, your board can authorize a repayment to you for this initial outlay. Remember, a charity may not distribute income to directors, officers, or individual members except as reasonable compensation for services received from them or as reimbursement for reasonable expenses, so it will be perfectly legitimate to reimburse you for these startup expenses. You could instead choose to make these the first tax-deductible donations to your organization and not be repaid.

From the start, you want to put in place financial checks and balances to be good stewards of the public's funds. The public is donating to this cause, so they have a right to expect that their funds will be used the right way.

Now, you wait. It can take three to four months to obtain certification of non-profit status from the IRS. It should be a bit quicker if you filed the EZ form.

Chapter 6 Action Items

~ Apply for your Employer Identification Number (EIN).
~ Determine whether you will need to file a longer Form 1023 or can qualify for the 1023-EZ Form.
~ Apply for 501(c)(3) status with the IRS.
~ Go to www.501Links.com/footnotes to get clickable links to all footnotes.

Chapter 7

Now Accepting Donations!

---◆O◆---

"G reat things are done by a series of small things brought together." - Vincent van Gogh

Initial Account or Money App

Once you have your name but are still awaiting your certification, you want to have at least one method of accepting donations to your organization. Donations will be tax-deductible to the donor retroactively to the date the corporation was formed,[1] so as long as you are SURE your organization will qualify, you can start accepting payments before you are official.

---

1. The corporation must file for 501 status with the IRS within 27 months of when it was formed:
   https://www.irs.gov/charities-non-profits/charitable-organizations/exempt
   -organizations-general-issues-deductibility-of-contributions-while-applicat
   ion-pending#:~:text=To%20be%20exempt%20under%20section,to%20the
   %20date%20of%20formation

Before receiving your nonprofit certification, you could set up a corporate bank account that would not qualify for nonprofit perks, or you could talk to a local community foundation about having an account under their nonprofit umbrella. You may want to set up a PayPal or Square account.[2] You NEVER want to commingle your personal funds with the organization's funds, so you need to separate funds from the start.

You will set up a business account (rather than a personal account) and choose "Nonprofit" as the type of organization. These payment service providers will ask if your organization is a corporation, when and where it was incorporated, and if it is a registered charity. They will also want the EIN number and your registered address (not a post office box).

Bank Account

Setting up a nonprofit bank account will be one of the final steps in establishing your organization. Banks typically require documentation from various stages of your nonprofit setup process to open an account.

The benefits of a nonprofit account compared to a standard business account can vary by bank. However, you will often find that nonprofit accounts require a lower minimum deposit to open, have a reduced minimum monthly balance required to avoid fees, and may charge less to send you paper statements. Be sure to shop different banks online or by phone ahead of time to find the one in your area that will charge the least amount of fees. You want your funds to support your programming, not be paid out in banking fees.

The first official board meeting should include discussion and a vote on how many check and bank account signers you will have. It is recommended that

---

2. Access the live links at 501Links.com/footnotes

you have **at least three unrelated authorized signers** and require two of the three to sign every check. Consider the location of the signers in relation to each other and to a bank branch, and whether it will be feasible for one of them to get a second signature when needed. The treasurer is almost always one of the designated signers. You may want to make a policy that checks only go out at certain intervals (weekly, every two weeks, or once a month) to give the signers time to get together.

The board may decide that since you are starting with an initial skeleton board, it is not practical to require two signers. You can start with one and have at least two backup signers. If this is the case, it is even more important to put in place checks and balances so the public and your donors can rest assured that mistakes will be caught, and you are being good stewards of their funds. Keep in mind that changing or removing authorized signers on a bank account can be a lengthy and challenging process. To avoid complications, choose signers who are trustworthy, are located nearby for easy access when signatures are needed, and are likely to remain on the board for several years.

Most banking and bill paying is done online these days, so carefully determine who has access to the online bank account and who has authorization to send out checks or transfer funds through the online account. What is the procedure for someone to receive that authorization? You may want to carefully define this policy and take a board vote on it.

Gather the following before heading to the bank:

1. All members who are designated to sign on the account – they will need to fill out signature cards (some members may go to the bank later to fill out their signature cards, but the bank will need to have all names when the account is opened)

2. Articles of incorporation/nonstock charter document signed by an officer of the corporation

3. EIN

4. Bylaws (these can be an early draft, voted in by the initial board, that mirror details in the articles of incorporation)

5. A list of board members and officers of the corporation

6. Minutes of the first official board meeting establishing: the board members, articles of incorporation, authorized signatories, and other governing documents

7. Proof of incorporation

8. The letter from the IRS confirming nonprofit status

Donations to your nonprofit are the lifeblood of the organization. It is important that your donors are thanked appropriately and within a week of the donation. If they donate online, set up an auto response email that quickly acknowledges their gift, but also have a system for sending a tax letter in the mail that lists the amount of their donation, the date of the gift, and a bit about how their funds will be used. If your donors feel their gift is appreciated and your organization is organized well enough to respond quickly, they will be more likely to donate again.

Chapter 7 Action Items

~ Open a money app or other corporate account that can begin accepting payments right away.

~ Set up a temporary corporate bank account while waiting for certification (optional).

~ Gather the necessary documents and officers, then head to the bank to open a nonprofit account.

~ Go to www.501Links.com/footnotes to get clickable links to all footnotes.

Chapter 8

Announcing Your Nonprofit

———◦———

"*A dream you dream alone is only a dream. A dream you dream together is reality.*" - John Lennon

Go Public

Press Releases

Once you have received your approval for 501(c)(3) status from the IRS, you are ready to be up and running. This includes sending out press releases to the local media announcing who you are and what you do. You can also "publish" your website (make it public) and set up your social media accounts. While you are waiting for your IRS certification, work on getting all of these ready to go "live" as soon as you are official.

Part of your public outreach should be sending press releases to local media outlets announcing your arrival. You can do an online search for sample press releases, and there is one for you here in Appendix 6. Be sure to introduce your nonprofit using the name, logo, branding, mission statement, who you intend to help and how. You may also want to include who is on the board, and any needs your organization has for volunteers, program participants, item donations, and funding. Give them contact information and a clear way to connect with your organization, and how to donate if they feel moved to do so. This should be a stretched version of your best elevator speech about your nonprofit.

When you email your press release, you should have a subject line that entices the receiver to open the email – maybe something like, "New Nonprofit Aims to ..." Some experts suggest copying and pasting your press release directly into the body of the email, so it is easy for the recipient to copy and paste it where they need it, and they are not wary of opening an attachment from someone they do not know. Start the email with a quick introduction of yourself and your organization, then add the press release. You can send the same email to multiple news outlets, but you may want to personalize your message a bit to each one. Be careful to proofread your message before sending, so you do not send Sally an email with the greeting, "Dear Bob."

Once you have researched local news outlets, you will want to keep an up-to-date list of the contact information and procedures to submit press releases for each so you can get the word out whenever your organization does something note-worthy. In future press releases, you may want to include a profile and photo for each person when adding new board or staff members. If you will be honoring a well-known member of the community at your upcoming event, this is a good way to advertise the event at the same time you recognize that person in the local media – and show that they have a connection to your organization. (Be sure to clear it with the honoree before sending it out to the media.) If your organization was recognized for an award, put that out in a press release so everyone can read about the good work you are doing. When you receive a grant from a foundation or corporation, include the name of the granting organization, express your gratitude publicly, and include details about the great program they are funding. (Again, be sure the organization allows you to publicize this grant.) Share these published press releases on your social media channels and your website to multiply the exposure.

Website

As soon as you are ready for the public to know you exist, publish your website. You may tweak and improve the site as you grow and change, but be sure there is at least a good landing page for people to test your credibility. It needs to look as good on a phone screen as it does on a laptop or tablet, and it should look professional with no glaring mistakes or typos.

You do not have to wait until all of the other pieces of your organization are in place to have your website up and running. Link it to a PayPal or other account so you are able to accept donations right away. (Donations are tax-deductible for the donor to the extent allowed by law retroactively to the date of the organization's legal formation [incorporation] as long as you have applied for 501(c)(3) status within 27 months of formation AND you do receive your tax deductible status.)

Social Media

Social media should be a part of your overall communications plan. It is essential for community engagement and brand awareness. It may also help generate donations and volunteers while broadening your reach. In addition to your website, people will look at your social media content if they want to learn more about your organization. Check out the social media pages for other nonprofits to get ideas about what to post (or what not to post), and see which posts are getting the most engagement.

As you know, there are many different platforms out there, with more being added every day. You should choose one or two platforms to start, and learn all that you can about posting on those platforms. Learn when to post for the highest effectiveness, who your intended target should be, and the type of post that does best on that particular platform. You do not need to try to be on all social media channels. It is best to have a consistent voice that is posting content at regular intervals, so assign one or two people that task.

With these outreach tools in place, you are now well prepared to spread the word about your nonprofit and connect with supporters. It is best if the board creates communications guidelines so all who are authorized to communicate on behalf of your organization are sharing the same information in the same way.

Congratulations!

You have now laid the groundwork for your nonprofit's success. Remember to find others who have the expertise you lack to fill in the gaps. Keep striving, stay transparent in your operations, and take a deep breath. You've got this!

Chapter 8 Action Items

~ Draft and distribute press releases.
~ Go live with your website.
~ Set up one or two social media platforms and research what works best on those platforms.
~ Go to www.501Links.com/footnotes to get clickable links to all footnotes.

Acknowledgments

Writing a book is never a solo endeavor, even though it sometimes feels that way with all of the alone time spent at a computer. I am grateful to those who contributed their time, insights, and support to help bring this book to life. A heartfelt thank you to my beta readers: Bonnie Adler, Suzanne Bigler, Stephanie Cory, Gigi Gaul, Keith Herrington, Debra Jost deTreville, Pam Meitner, and Robert Whetzel for their valuable feedback, which helped refine and strengthen this book. Your keen eyes and thoughtful suggestions made all the difference.

I want to thank 100 Covers for designing a cover that truly captures the essence of the book. Your creative vision brought my work to life in a way I could not have done alone. I also want to acknowledge Atticus book formatting software and Pubfunnels for providing author-friendly platforms. Atticus made it easy for me to write my manuscript and then format it into book form, while Pubfunnels hosts my website and the funnels that allow the footnotes and incorporation papers to be easily accessed. I would also like to note the helpful brainstorming and editing support from ChatGPT, which allowed me to refine my ideas and enhance this book's clarity.

Finally, to every aspiring nonprofit founder who picks up this book – thank you for your dedication to making a difference. It is my hope that these pages guide you on your journey to creating meaningful impact in your community.

Appendix 1

Elevator Pitch

Introduce Yourself: When introducing yourself, always look the person directly in the eye (not averting your gaze but also not staring them down), smile, and, if shaking hands, be sure to give a nice, firm handshake. The intent is to show your confidence (even if you have to "fake it 'til you make it") with a firm but not crushing handshake. I can't tell you how many times men have shaken my hand with the "dead fish" handshake where they barely touch my hand. I'm not sure if they were trying to be deferential to a woman, or if they shake everyone's hand that way, but it was very distracting and not a good first impression.

Smile, give your full name, and you may want to add the name of the organization you are representing. If you have met the person before, but they may not remember you or may not remember your name, tell them your name again. This lets them off the hook from trying to remember how they know you and what your name is so they can concentrate on the important information you have to share with them. A welcoming introduction sets the stage for a friendly, natural conversation.

Get Straight to the Important Details: You are on a tight timeline to deliver your message. Try to fit your core pitch into a 30-60 second time limit. If the person engages with you and asks questions, you can deliver more details then. When writing it, try to stay to about 100 words for the initial pitch.

- Start with a surprising fact or figure related to your cause.

- Give a quick overview of your nonprofit's mission. The mission should clearly state the problem you are trying to address.

- Give the story behind why this organization exists. Did your relative have a disease that has not gotten the research and recognition you feel it needs? Are there too many children going to school without shoes that fit them? What is the reason for YOUR passion for this cause?

- Give a few statistics you have learned about the need for your services.

- What programs are you offering that will help alleviate these problems?

- Explain how a donor can make an impact.

As your organization grows and evolves, the elevator pitch will change, too. You can add a specific story of how someone's life was improved with the help you provided. The statistics you give them can be directly related to your organization's success rates.

Example (1st Draft – This Version May Be Used When There is More Time)[1]:

Did you know that women make up only 25% of the U.S. Senate and 29% of the U.S. House of Representatives? Ready to Run Delaware is a local nonprofit with

---

1. The example here is for an actual nonprofit I started. It qualified to be a 501(c)(3) organization because it was instructing people on how to run a political campaign. It was not endorsing any particular party or candidate.

a mission to prepare women to run a successful political campaign, helping each woman find her voice and get a seat at the table.

I have talked to a lot of people who are not happy with our political landscape, but they feel as if there is not much they can do about it. Many of them are strong, smart, educated, capable women who just don't know the first thing about running a campaign or serving in a political seat.

Women have had the right to vote for more than 100 years, and yet they make up about a quarter of our Congressional seat holders. Research shows that women make government more transparent, inclusive, and accessible. If we start by helping women get a seat at the local government level, that will lead to broader roles in the future.

Ready to Run Delaware is offering six two-hour classes starting next month. We have lined up a fantastic slate of speakers, from those who have worked in the White House to some who were just elected to their first terms in state government.

We need your help to attract more participants – women who are considering running for office but who may need a little help getting started. We also need funds to offset our costs for our meeting room rental, travel reimbursement for speakers coming from Washington, technology costs for Zoom and our website, advertising, and other costs.

Example (Edited Draft – Short Time Frame):

Did you know that, even though women have had the right to vote for more than 100 years, women make up only about a quarter of the U.S. Congress? I am with Ready to Run Delaware, a local nonprofit with a mission to get more women a seat at the table.

We are starting classes next month to prepare women to run a political campaign. We have about 20 speakers, all with first-hand knowledge, who will help these women get started.

Your donation can help local women learn how to run for office and where to turn for support once they win – whether running for the local school board, county council, or state senate.

Appendix 2

Sample Meeting Minutes

―――――◄O►―――――

B elow is a sample of meeting minutes for a specific meeting. When listing those in attendance, they may be listed in a grid with a column to check for those "In Attendance" and one to check for those members/directors who are absent. Another option is for the secretary to look around the room and list those in attendance (as below), then compare that to the list of all members to find and list who was missing.

These sample minutes are for an organization that has been in existence for many years, so they are updating the bylaws to more accurately reflect what they have decided the rules for attendance should be and how this should be tracked and recorded. They also want to spell out the role and responsibility of the chair emerita – the person who is the immediate past chair. (Note that "emerita" is the feminine form of this title so a man would be chair emeritus.)

Meetings work best if the meeting materials, including committee reports with updates since the last meeting, the financials, the meeting agenda, and any other items that will be up for discussion are sent out to all members at least a few days before the meeting. It should be made clear to all members that part of their obligation in serving on the board is to read through and be familiar with the materials before coming to the meeting. This way, precious meeting time is not spent getting all members up to speed, and the time can be better spent on specific questions and discussion, especially if the item requires a board vote.

You will see when there is a vote on something, one person will move (or make a motion) to approve the item as discussed, then another member will second the motion. There may be further discussion about the item before a vote. The board then votes, and, if a simple majority (at least 51% of the members voting at a meeting where a quorum is present) approves the vote, the "motion carries" (or passes). Your bylaws may specify the types of votes requiring a supermajority rather than only a simple majority to pass. A supermajority may be 3/5 (60%), 2/3 (66.67%), 3/4 (75%), or some other amount larger than 51%. You will want these supermajority votes to be required in order to change things like your bylaws or mission, removing a board member, selling significant assets, dissolving the organization, and other major changes made to the nonprofit.

When they discuss the Annual Campaign (the fundraising effort that takes place each year during a specified time frame), they mention "unrestricted funds." This means donations that are not designated for a specific purpose by the donor. This gives the nonprofit the flexibility to use the money where it's most needed.

Also notice that this organization holds board retreat meetings annually to do strategic planning. Many times, regular board meetings are so full with items that need to be acted on right away, there is no time to think or plan long term. A multi-hour or multi-day retreat to really focus on the future is a good idea.

XYZ Charity, Inc.

Board of Trustees
May 4, 2024 6:00 p.m.
Meeting Minutes

In attendance: Mary Smith (Chair), Ashley Martin (Vice Chair), Sally Hartley (Treasurer), Melissa Star (Secretary), Abigail Vander (at-large), Nancy Bentley (Events Chair), Barbara Barr (Volunteer & Database Coordinator)

Absent: Kelly McBride (Governance Chair), Mimi Jones (Chair Emerita)

Meeting was called to order at 6:03 p.m.

Meeting Minutes

There were no suggested changes to the April 12, 2024 meeting minutes. Nancy Bentley made a motion that was seconded by Melissa Star to approve the minutes. Motion carried – minutes approved.

Financials – Sally Hartley

Sally reported that our endowment account balance as of March 31 was $231,380. Our operating account balance at ABC Bank was $67,853.

During this year, we have added $81,569 from the annual event and donations.

Sally will be correcting revenue by the next board meeting. Funds were incorrectly shown in the "A County" account that should have been in the "B County" account. She will also reconcile the Extra Account Fund, as she does not believe the balance listed in today's financials is correct. She will work with Richard Little at ABC Bank to reconcile.

Committee Reports

Volunteers & Database – Barbara Barr reported that there were eight new volunteers since our last board of trustees meeting. The B County Fashion Show contributed five new volunteers to that number. New links have been created for the upcoming events.

Database access was discussed – It was agreed that an official policy for access should be written. The executive committee should determine who has access to the donor database and the level of access granted. Different levels of access include: view, create reports, input data, and manipulate data. The data needs to be safe and secure. Further discussion included the recommendation of hiring someone for five to eight hours a week to be trained by Barbara Barr to be a database access assistant to provide some institutional knowledge continuity when volunteers change roles. No formal vote was taken on hiring this position, but there was agreement that we should further explore this option.

Annual Event Ceremony – Nancy Bentley reported that 100 people have signed up for the Annual Event Ceremony on May 12. Many registrants participated in the sponsor-a-student option when purchasing a ticket to the ceremony to underwrite student attendance at the event. Monday, May 9 is the deadline for reservations for the buses. Vicky (our part-time paid admin) will not be able to attend the event. Volunteer Cathy Anton is working on flowers we can give away after the event. Ashley Martin will be arriving early and Kelly McBride and Melissa Star have volunteered to work the event. Photographer Jane has been confirmed.

Annual Campaign – The year-end mail campaign was very successful, raising nearly $20,000 in unrestricted funds.

Governance – Kelly provided a report on the recent activity of the governance committee at their April 25, 2024 meeting. She was unable to attend tonight's meeting. They are recommending the following bylaws changes. (These changes will require a supermajority vote.)

1. Currently reads: Trustees are expected to participate in at least 70% of the monthly meetings and other events sponsored by XYZ. Proposed language: **Trustees are expected to participate in at least 70% of the monthly meetings. It is also expected that trustees will attend as many XYZ-sponsored events as possible.**

   Motion to approve was made by Sally Hartley, seconded by Melissa Star. Motion carried.

2. New language to be added to bylaws: **The Secretary shall track trustee attendance at all monthly board meetings and bring any issues to the attention of the board chair and the governance committee chair.**

   Motion to approve was made by Barbara Barr, seconded by Ashley Martin. Motion carried.

3. New language to be added to bylaws: **The chair emerita is the immediate previous board of trustees chair. This person is a voting member of the board and executive committee for two years only. They will provide institutional knowledge and help guide the current Chair. They should attend 70% of the board meetings to remain a voting member of the board and executive committee.**

   Motion to approve was made by Nancy Bentley, seconded by Sally Harley. Motion carried.

The governance committee recommends making the following changes to the board structure that will be presented to the board of trustees at the June 15 board retreat:

1. Move archivist responsibilities to the secretary.

2. Secure an assistant for the Secretary to help with additional responsibilities and to serve as next in line for main Secretary.

3. Change the name of the "media relations committee" to the "communications committee" which will be tasked with publicity/press releases, public communication, invites, e-blasts, and the newsletter. This committee will also communicate volunteer opportunities.

4. Look at adding new policies and procedures such as a contract policy (who in the organization is approved to sign a contract on behalf of the organization), expenses policy (dollar amount over which expenses must be pre-approved and by whom, types and amounts of expenses that may be reimbursed, how to submit an expense for reimbursement, etc.), confidentiality policy, and others.

5. Discuss the need for vice chair positions on all committees for succession planning.

After feedback is provided by the board of trustees, Kelly McBride will reconvene a meeting of the governance committee.

Upcoming Events:

May 12 – Grants Event 5:45 p.m. to 7:30 p.m.
May 17 – Garden Party at Cathy Keir's home 5:30 p.m. to 7:30 p.m.
June 15 – Next Board Meeting 4:00 p.m. to 6:30 p.m.
September 28 – Annual Breakfast 7:45 a.m.

Meeting was adjourned at 8:04 p.m.

Appendix 3

Mission & Vision Statements

———————◄○►———————

M ission and vision statements are usually mentioned together, but each serves a distinct purpose. Both require deep thought, discussion, and careful wordsmithing. They should be **clearly defined, broad enough to allow for future growth,** yet **focused enough to provide direction** – avoid trying to be everything to everyone. These statements form the backbone of your nonprofit's work. However, know that if your nonprofit outgrows its initial mission and vision statements at some point, you can always revise them later.

Your Mission Statement: Defining Your Focus Today

A mission statement is the clear, concise **declaration of your nonprofit's focus today and every day**. It's what guides your board, staff, and volunteers, ensuring everyone is on the same path heading in the same direction. Your statement should be succinct and to the point, while being very clear as to your intent. It should be narrow enough to give your organization focus and purpose but broad enough to allow for growth. Try to keep it simple and direct enough that it is easy to memorize.

Your mission should be:

- Succinct and specific, yet flexible enough to allow for future growth.

- Focused, so your organization stays on track.

- A guidepost, helping you stay true to your purpose, especially in difficult times.

While flexibility is important, be very careful not to let others coax you into stretching your mission to be something you never intended. This "mission creep" can happen when certain funders tempt you with promised donations that are tied to doing work outside your original scope. Your board must be prepared to stick to the mission, resisting pressures to steer the program off course or expand the mission due to offers of funding for things not quite "on mission."

Your Vision Statement: Imagining the Future

Your vision statement is **your nonprofit's hope for the future** – the aspirational goal. It is a "big picture" dream of the long-term impact you strive to achieve. You may even aim to "fix" the problems and put yourself out of business. For example: *"Our vision is to eliminate hunger in our country."*

Your vision should be:

- Ambitious but relevant – not a vague wish for a better world.

- A source of inspiration for your team and supporters.

- Clearly connected to your nonprofit's mission and work.

Brainstorming Your Mission and Vision Statements

If you are just starting out, here is a step-by-step approach to help you craft strong statements:

1. Start with "Why?"

   a. What problem are you trying to solve?

   b. Who do you serve, and why does this matter?

   c. What inspired you to start this nonprofit?

2. Define Your Mission (What You Do Today)

   Your mission statement should answer:

   a. Who do you serve? (a specific population or cause)

   b. What problem do you address?

   c. How do you address it? (programs, services, advocacy, etc.)

   Example Mission Statement:

   "We provide free financial literacy education and mentorship to low-income high school students, empowering them to build a secure financial future."

3. Envision the Future (Your Long-Term Impact)

   Think about the big picture:

   a. If your nonprofit is successful, what will change?

   b. What would the world look like if your mission were fully accomplished?

   Example Vision Statement:

   "A world where every young person, regardless of background, has the financial knowledge and resources to achieve economic stability and success."

4. Involve Others in the Process

Engage potential board members, volunteers, and advisors in brain-storming sessions. Their insights can help refine your statements and ensure they resonate with your target audience.

5. Keep It Short and Clear

a. The mission statement should ideally be one to two sentences.

b. Your vision statement should be a single sentence or a short paragraph.

6. Test & Refine

Once you draft your statements, ask:

a. Are they clear and specific?

b. Do they inspire and guide action?

c. Would a stranger immediately understand what we do?

While crafting your mission and vision, also think about the long-term vision for your nonprofit.

- Will this be a perpetual nonprofit, or do you aim to accomplish your mission within a set timeframe?

- Do you envision keeping it small and local, or do you have plans for growth?

- While you can adjust these plans over time, getting everyone on the same page early on is valuable.

Looking for Inspiration?

Do an online search for examples of nonprofit mission and vision statements to see how organizations similar to yours articulate their purpose. This can help spark ideas and ensure your statements are both impactful and unique.

Appendix 4

Sample Articles of Incorporation

The articles of incorporation may be called different things in different states. They are also known as a certificate of incorporation, a certificate of formation, or a nonstock charter. A nonprofit has a "nonstock" charter because there is no stock issued and no dividends or income may be distributed to directors, officers, or individual members except as reasonable compensation for services rendered. The charter or certificate is the official document that states the name of the corporation, the registered address, the purpose of the nonprofit, and how the nonprofit may operate. It gives details about the board (terms, number of members, etc.), details about what must be included in the bylaws and how they may be amended, and spells out what happens if the organization is dissolved. For an organization to qualify for exemption with the IRS, there are certain provisions that must be included in the organizing documents.

Consult IRS.gov to be sure your documents are in compliance.[1]

Under the "Conditions of Membership" in number 5, include that your organization is a nonprofit with the sole purpose being for public benefit. The IRS requires that you also include:

1. That your nonprofit will only benefit charitable causes

2. The earnings will not be used for personal benefit

3. Assets of the nonprofit will not be distributed to the owners or directors upon dissolution

Your registered agent must be located at a physical address in the state of incorporation.

---

1. ("Charity – Required Provisions for Organizing Documents" [Reviewed or Updated August 19, 2024]) IRS.gov:
   https://www.irs.gov/charities-non-profits/charitable-organizations/charity-required-provisions-for-organizing-documents

<u>Sample[2]</u>:

CERTIFICATE OF INCORPORATION

OF

XYZ Charity, Inc.

XYZ Charity, Inc. is a charitable nonstock corporation organized and existing under the laws of the State of Delaware, hereby certifies that:

ARTICLE I

The name of the Corporation is XYZ Charity, Inc. (the "Corporation").

ARTICLE II

The registered address of the Corporation in the State of Delaware is 123 Main Street, Wilmington, DE 19808.

The name of the registered agent at such address is The Incorporation Company, Inc.

ARTICLE III

---

2. This is a sample and should not be used verbatim without consulting an attorney in your state of incorporation. The Articles of Incorporation should not be used by your organization without them being understood by at least some board members who can assure they are applied correctly to your organization.

The Corporation shall be a nonstock corporation as defined in Section 114(d)(3) of the General Corporation Law of the State of Delaware and, as such, shall not be authorized to issue capital stock. The conditions of membership in the Corporation shall be set forth in the bylaws of the Corporation (the "Bylaws").

The purposes of the Corporation are:

1. To operate exclusively for charitable, scientific, literary, or educational purposes.

2. To receive and maintain a fund or funds of personal property, and, subject to the restrictions and limitations hereinafter set forth, to use and apply the whole or any part of the income therefrom and the principal thereof exclusively for charitable, scientific, literary, or educational purposes, either directly or by contributions to organizations that qualify as exempt organizations under Section 501(c)(3) of the Internal Revenue Code of 1986, as amended (the "Code").

3. To engage in any and all activities incidental to the foregoing purposes, except as specifically restricted herein.

<u>ARTICLE IV</u>

At all times, and notwithstanding merger, consolidation, reorganization, termination, dissolution, or winding up of the Corporation, voluntarily or involuntarily, or by operation of law or any other provision thereof:

1. No part of the net earnings of the Corporation shall inure to the benefit of any member, trustee, director, or officer of the Corporation, or any private individual (except that reasonable compensation may be paid for services rendered to or for the Corporation affecting one or more of its purposes), and no member, trustee, director, or officer of

the Corporation, or any private individual, shall be entitled to share in the distribution of any of the corporate assets upon dissolution of the Corporation.

2. No substantial part of the activities of the Corporation shall consist of the carrying on of propaganda or otherwise attempting to influence legislation, and the Corporation shall not participate in or intervene in (including by publication or distribution of statements) any political campaign on behalf of (or in opposition to) any candidate for public office.

3. The Corporation shall not be operated for the purpose of carrying on a trade or business for profit.

4. The Corporation shall distribute its income for each taxable year at such time and in such manner as not to subject the Corporation to tax on undistributed income imposed by Section 4942 of the Code.

5. The Corporation shall not engage in any act of self-dealing as defined in Section 4941 of the Code.

6. The Corporation shall not retain any excess business holdings as defined in Section 4943 of the Code.

7. The Corporation shall not make any investments in such a manner as to subject the Corporation to tax under Section 4944 of the Code.

8. The Corporation shall not make any taxable expenditures as defined in Section 4945 of the Code.

9. Notwithstanding any other provision of this certificate, the Corporation shall not conduct or carry on any activities not permitted to be conducted or carried on by an organization exempt under Section 501(c)(3)

of the Code, or by an organization contributions to which are deductible under Section 170(c)(2) of the Code.

10. Upon the dissolution of the Corporation or the winding up of its affairs, after paying or making provision for the payment of all liabilities and obligations of the Corporation, the assets of the Corporation shall be distributed exclusively to charitable, scientific, literary, or educational organizations which would then qualify under the provisions of Section 501(c)(3) of the Code.

ARTICLE V

The Corporation shall be financed through contributions, gifts, grants, donations, bequests, devises, benefactions, and other voluntary transfers of property.

ARTICLE VI

The Corporation shall have perpetual existence.

ARTICLE VII

The business and affairs of the Corporation shall be managed by or under the direction of the governing body of the Corporation. The governing body shall be known as the Board of Directors, and individual members of the Board of Directors shall be known as directors. The number of directors which shall constitute the whole board shall be fixed by the Board of Directors in the manner provided in the Bylaws, but in no event shall the number be less than five (5) or more than twenty-one (21).

The Board of Directors shall be divided into three classes, as nearly equal in number as possible, as follows: (A) one class initially consisting of one or two directors ("Class I"), the initial term of which shall expire at the first annual board meeting ("Annual Meeting") to be held after the date hereof; (B) a second class initially consisting of one or two directors ("Class II"), the initial term of which shall expire at the second Annual Meeting to be held after the date hereof, and (C) a third class initially consisting of one or two directors ("Class III"), the initial term of which shall expire at the third Annual Meeting to be held after the date hereof, with each class to hold office until its successors are elected and qualified. At each Annual Meeting, the successors of the members of the class of directors whose term expires at that meeting shall be elected to hold office for a term expiring at the third succeeding Annual Meeting. On the date hereof, the Board shall consist of (i) Mary A. Smith and Ronald D. Whitmyer in Class I, (ii) Robert H. Webb in Class II, and (iii) Lisa L. Martin and Beverly Brick in Class III.

Directors may serve for up to three successive three-year terms (for a total of nine successive years) and may be elected to further terms following a two-year break in service as a director; provided, however, that for purposes of calculating the number of years of service by any director, any period of time during which the director also serves as an officer of the Corporation, any period during which the immediate past President of the Corporation serves as an *ex-officio* member of the Board of Directors in accordance with the Bylaws of the Corporation, and any period of less than six months between the time of appointment and the next Annual Meeting, directors whose term expires at such Annual Meeting shall not be counted in determining eligibility to serve as a director. At each Annual Meeting, directors whose term expires at such Annual Meeting shall stand for re-election unless such director is not eligible for re-election due to exceeding the number of successive terms for which a director may be elected or due to failure to meet the qualifications set forth in the Bylaws. Any vacancies on the Board of Directors, whether by death, resignation, removal, retirement, disqualification, or other cause, and any newly created directorship, shall be filled in the manner provided in the Bylaws. The Bylaws shall specify the number of directors necessary to constitute a quorum for the transaction of business at any meeting of the Board of Directors. Any director of the Corporation may be removed from office, with or without cause, by the affirmative vote of a majority of members of the Board of Directors present at any meeting thereof at which a quorum is present.

ARTICLE VIII

The Board of Directors shall have the power to make, adopt, amend, or repeal, from time to time, the Bylaws.

ARTICLE IX

The members of the Corporation as such shall have no voting rights and no separate vote of members shall be required on any matter, except with respect to any matter where a member vote is required by law and such member vote cannot be eliminated by provision of the certificate of incorporation. If and to the extent that a vote of members is required by law on any matter and cannot be eliminated by provision of the certificate of incorporation, the vote of the Board of Directors shall be the vote of the members on such matters.

ARTICLE X

A director of the Corporation shall not be personally liable to the Corporation or its members for monetary liability for breach of fiduciary duty as a director, except for liability (i) for any breach of the director's duty of loyalty to the Corporation or its members, (ii) for acts or omissions not in good faith or which involved intentional misconduct or a knowing violation of law, or (iii) for any transaction from which the director derived an improper personal benefit.

The private property, both real and personal, of the directors or officers of the Corporation, shall not be subject to the payment of the corporate debts to any extent whatsoever.

The Corporation shall indemnify its members, directors, officers, employees, and agents to the fullest extent permitted by applicable law.

ARTICLE XI

Upon dissolution of the Corporation, the Board of Directors shall: (a) pay or make provision for the payment of all of the Corporation's liabilities; (b) return, transfer, or convey (or make provision therefor) all assets held by the Corporation upon condition requiring such return, transfer, or conveyance in the event of dissolution of the Corporation; and (c) dispose of the Corporation's remaining assets exclusively for the purposes of the Corporation or distribute the assets to an organization or organizations organized and operated exclusively for charitable, educational, scientific, religious, or literary purposes as shall, at that time, qualify for exemption under Section 501(c)(3) of the Code, as the Board of Directors shall determine, provided that none of such assets shall be distributed to any individual or any entity for profit. Any such assets not so disposed of shall be disposed of by the circuit court of the city or county in which the principal office of the Corporation is then located, to be used exclusively for purposes that are charitable, educational, scientific, religious, or literary within the meaning of Section 501(c)(3) of the Code or to an organization or organizations organized and operated exclusively for such purposes.

ARTICLE XII

The Corporation reserves the right to amend, alter, or change any provision contained in this Certificate of Incorporation in the manner now or hereafter prescribed by applicable statute, and all rights conferred herein are granted subject to this reservation.

The name and address of the Incorporator is:

Name: _____

Address: _____

_____

The undersigned duly authorized officer of XYZ Charity, Inc. has executed this Certificate of Incorporation on this 24th day of April, 2025.

XYZ Charity, Inc.

X_____

By: Lisa L. Martin
President

Appendix 5

Applying for EIN

The IRS online tool used to apply for an Employer Identification Number (EIN) is available Monday through Friday from 7:00 a.m. to 10:00 p.m. Eastern time at the IRS.gov website.[1] The instructions below will help you navigate the application process.

1. When you go to the IRS.gov EIN application site, it will ask that you read the "Important Information" then click "Begin Application."

2. Select "Corporations" then "Continue."

3. Select "Corporation" on the second page then "Continue."

4. "Continue" again to confirm your previous selection.

5. Select "Started a new business" as your reason for applying for the EIN.

6. Fill in YOUR name and YOUR Social Security Number.

---

1. Apply for EIN:
   https://sa.www4.irs.gov/modiein/individual/index.jsp

7. Choose whether you are a corporate officer or a third party applying on behalf of the corporation. If you are applying as a third party, you will need a signed form from the taxpayer authorizing you to act on behalf of the corporation.

8. Enter the corporation's physical address (this can be your home address, if applicable). In the designated field, you may provide your name or another person's name if you want IRS correspondence directed to a specific individual. Alternatively, you can leave this field blank to have mail addressed directly to the corporation. If your mailing or registered address differs from the physical address, check the box at the bottom of the page to provide that information. Hit "Continue" and it will verify the postal version of the address. Click on their database version if it is correct.

9. On the next page you will fill in the legal name of the corporation (the official name under which it was incorporated), the "Doing Business As" or DBA name (if applicable), the county and state where the corporation is incorporated, the state where the articles of incorporation are filed, the date (month and year) when the corporation was started, and the *closing month* of your accounting year. (If your fiscal year is July 1-June 30, the answer to this question will be June.)

10. Answer the yes or no questions on the next page:
    A. Do you own a large vehicle?
    B. Does your business involve gambling?
    C. Do you need to file a Form 720 (quarterly Federal Excise Tax Return)?
    D. Do you manufacture alcohol, tobacco, or firearms?
    E. Do you have or expect to have any employees who will receive W-2 Forms from this corporation in the next 12 months? (Forms W-2 require additional filings with the IRS.)

11. Choose the type of business you will be running from the list: accommodations (casino hotel, hotel, or motel), construction, finance, food service, health care, insurance, manufacturing, real estate, rental & leasing, retail, social assistance, transportation, warehousing, wholesale, or other. Each option has a few examples next to it.

12. If you choose "other," there are more options to narrow that down on the next page: consulting, manufacturing, organization (such as religious, environmental, social or civic, athletic, etc.), rental, repair, sell goods, service, or other (fill in the blank here).

13. If you choose "organization" from the list above, it will ask you to narrow that down further: athletic, conservation, environmental, fundraising, homeowners association, religious, social or civic, or other (fill in the blank here).

14. Lastly, it will ask how you would like to receive your EIN Confirmation Letter. The options are "Online" which requires you to have Adobe Reader (which you can download from their link) or "By Mail." If you choose online, you can view, print, and save the letter immediately – it will not be mailed. If you choose to have it mailed to you, it could take up to four weeks to receive it. Keep the letter in a safe place with the rest of the formation and governing documents of the organization. You will need your EIN for tax filings and other official business for the rest of your nonprofit's existence.

Remember, this site will time you out after 15 minutes, so be prepared with all of your answers ahead of time.

Appendix 6

Sample Press Release

---◄O►---

FOR IMMEDIATE RELEASE (3/8/25)

Contact: May Smith, Executive Director
Phone Number: 303-555-1212
Email: info@ABCLit.org
Website: www.ABCLit.org

New Nonprofit Launches to Support Early Childhood Literacy

ABC Lit Aims to Help Children Ages 4-8 Build Strong Reading Skills

Everytown, MD – March 8, 2025 – ABC Lit, a newly established nonprofit organization, is excited to announce its launch in Everytown, MD, dedicated to enhancing early literacy skills for ages 4-8. In collaboration with local public schools, ABC Lit will offer specialized reading support programs designed to help young students develop foundational literacy skills.

The organization's trained volunteers will work directly with students, dedicating two hours per session, twice a week, to engage children in personalized reading activities. ABC Lit's mission is to empower children with the literacy tools they need to succeed academically and confidently in the future.

"We believe that early literacy is the key to lifelong success, and by investing in young learners at this critical stage, we are giving them the tools to thrive both inside and outside the classroom," said May Smith, Executive Director of ABC Lit. "Our volunteers are passionate about supporting Everytown's children, and we are excited to work hand-in-hand with the local schools to create a lasting impact."

The program will be available to children attending local public schools in Everytown, MD. By working closely with the teachers and school staff, ABC Lit will tailor its reading interventions to meet the individual needs of each child, ensuring that every student receives the personalized attention they deserve.

ABC Lit is actively recruiting volunteers who are interested in making a difference in the community. Volunteers will receive training and guidance to work effectively with children and ensure the highest quality of support for their reading development. To volunteer, visit ABCLit.org.

The nonprofit's mission extends beyond just improving reading skills – it aims to foster a love of learning and build the confidence of young readers. By creating an engaging and supportive environment, ABC Lit hopes to inspire children to embrace reading as a lifelong skill and passion.

For more information on ABC Lit, including how to get involved or donate, please visit www.ABCLit.org.

Resources

If you found this book to be helpful in creating your nonprofit organization, **please consider leaving an honest review on Amazon**. This will help others who are not sure how to get started setting up their new nonprofit decide if this is the book they need. You know how helpful it is to read reviews when considering a purchase. I thank you in advance for taking the time to leave a review. There is a direct link to the review page in the footnotes document (501Links.com/footnotes).

Nonprofit Setup Simplified along with my previous book *So, You Want to Start a Nonprofit, Now What?* were developed as resources for nonprofit founders. The **501Guide.com** website provides access to additional nonprofit information and valuable tools.

Michele Whetzel is a nonprofit consultant who may be reached through the 501 Guide website or by email at mlwhetzel@501Guide.com.

About the Author

Michele Whetzel has spent more than 20 years in the non-profit sector, serving on 14 boards and numerous committees. Her leadership experience spans executive roles from treasurer to board chair, with expertise in fundraising, governance, grants, and events. As a nonprofit consultant, she brings a well-rounded perspective on building and sustaining successful organizations.

Passionate about connecting people with opportunities and championing causes that empower communities, Michele values ethical leadership, transparency, and lifelong learning. She holds a B.S. degree in Finance with a minor in Economics from the University of Delaware and has pursued advanced coursework toward a Masters of Taxation at Widener University. In 2020, she earned her *Preparing to Be a Corporate Director* certification from Harvard Business School.

Michele and her husband, Robert, live in Delaware, while their two adult children now call Nashville, Tennessee home. She welcomes connections and conversations. Reach out to her at **mlwhetzel@501Guide.com**.